Table of Contents

Prologue
The Wisdom That Raised Me

Introduction
She Didn't Just Teach Me—She Transformed Me

Dedication

"From Her Heart to My Spirit"

Part One: Rooted in Worth

1. I Am Not a Rug
Boundaries, Self-Worth & Refusing to Be Walked Over

2. Stay Clean in Spirit and Body
Hygiene as a Sacred Practice

3. You Are a Magnet
Desire, Attraction, and Not Begging

4. When the Chest Feels Heavy
Discernment and Spirit-Led Decisions

5. You Are Your Own Savior
Self-Agency & Ancestral Backup

6. Walk Barefoot, Listen to the Wind
Nature as Divine Messenger

7. Your Star Will Burn Them
Spiritual Authority & Chosen Identity

8. Don't Shrink for Nobody
Authenticity vs. Conformity

9. They'll Try to Imprint You
Protection from Jealous Spirits

10. Take a Break, Then Fly
Avoiding Burnout and Rest as Rebellion

Part Two: Strategic Spirit

11. Fast When It's Good Too
Gratitude as a Lifestyle

12. When They Can't Empathize, Walk Like Royalty
Inner Nobility in the Face of Rejection

13. Mind Your Own Million
Discipline, Focus, and Financial Power

14. You Are the Altar
Stop Searching Outside of Yourself

15. Never Sabotage Yourself
The Sacredness of Self-Trust

16. Your Light Triggers Them
Energetic Boundaries and Awareness

17. The Real Battle is Psychological
Staying Rooted in Truth

18. Don't Fight Back Unless It's Personal
Strategic Defense

19. Keep Track and Stay in the Light
Spiritual Journaling & Recall

20. You Are Already Complete
 No Need for External Validation

Part Three: A Legacy That Lives

21. Final Words from Grandma
A Letter to Her Legacy (You)

Bonus:

- The Legacy Continues With You
- She Was the Root—I Am the Bloom
- Final Dedication
- Aha Moment
- Why This Book Now, and How It Can Benefit You
- Words of Encouragement
- *Final Declaration*
- *Conclusion: The Legacy Continues With You*
- *Final Conclusion: She Was the Root—I Am the Bloom*
- *Bonus Epilogue: The Woman I Never Met—But Always Knew*
- *Final Message to the Reader*
- *A Love Letter to the Grandmothers*

"I could have ignored the call, but I chose to listen to the voice of my angel— even when no one else heard her, I did.
And that has made all the difference."

Rev. Dr. Marie Brevil

Prologue: The Wisdom That Raised Me

This is not just a book. It is a transmission.
A soul-to-soul conversation passed down through blood, bone, and breath.
A woven thread of whispers that began long before I arrived here—carried by a woman who saw storms, survived them, and still dared to rise with grace.

My grandmother. My Grann Cheri. My Manman.
She was my first temple. My first embrace.
My first peace, joy, abundance, and love.
My first mirror. My first moral lesson.
My first teacher, my guru.
My first guide in a world that often teaches us to forget ourselves.
She didn't raise me with fluff or fantasy.
She raised me with truth.
With oil and fire.
With a broom and a prayer. Cori shells and spells
With boundary and backbone.
Herbal leaves and bones.

She raised me to stand when the world would rather I kneel.
Her words weren't just advice—they were armor.
Her presence wasn't just comforting—it was activating.
She didn't just tell me I mattered—she showed me how to live like it.

What you are about to read is not fiction.
It's not a lesson in tradition.
It's a reclamation.
A remembrance.

A collection of the sacred things she poured into me —when the world tried to strip me down.

Each chapter is a doorway.
Each lesson is a legacy.

And every sentence holds a vibration meant to meet you right where you are and lift you into where you were always meant to be.

This is for every child who was made to feel too loud, too much, too sensitive, too defiant.

This is for the ones who are now grown, carrying invisible scars and wondering where their strength went.

Let me be clear:

You are not lost.
You are not broken.
You are not behind.
You are simply ready—now—to remember.

Let this be your remembering.

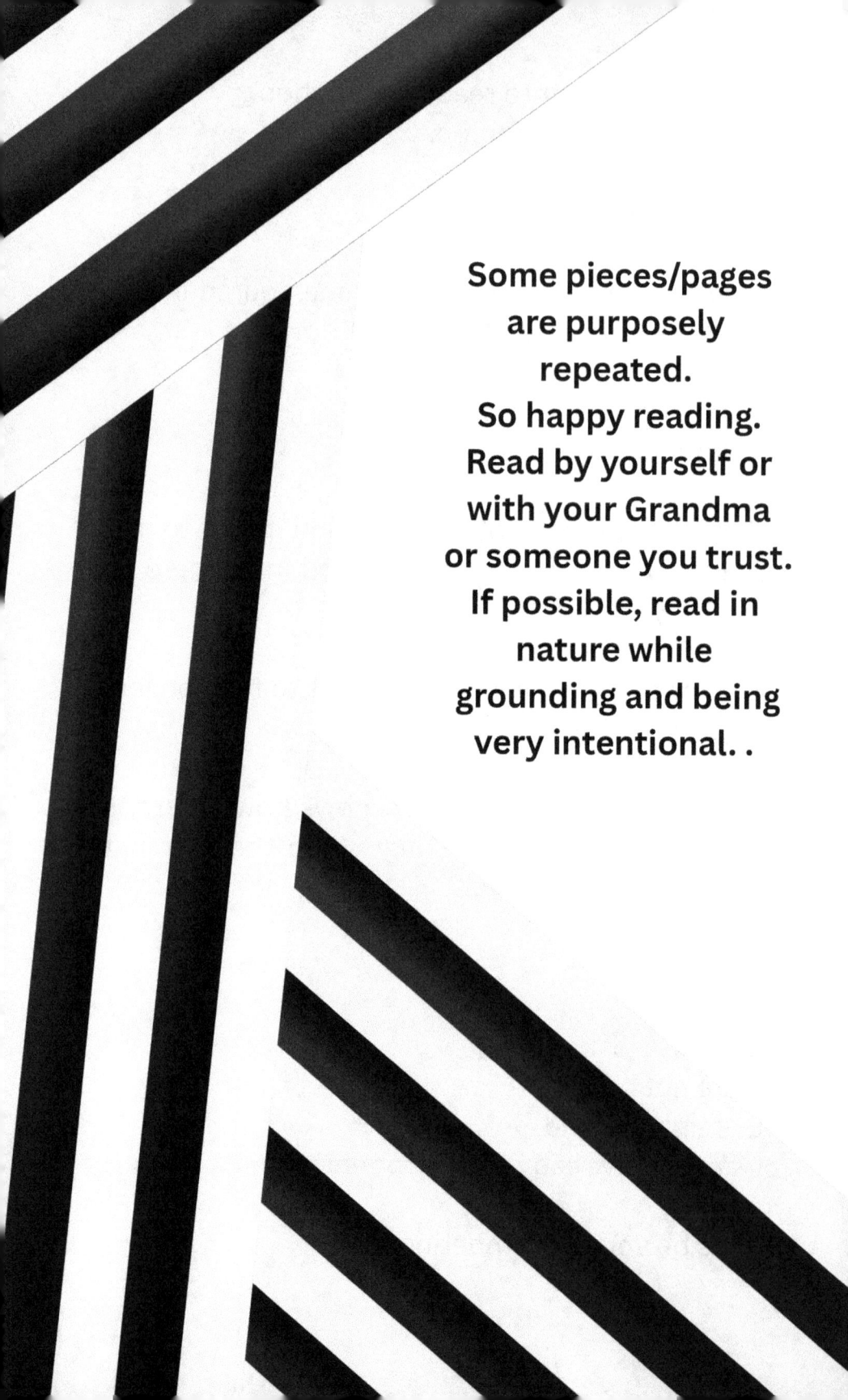

Some pieces/pages are purposely repeated.
So happy reading.
Read by yourself or with your Grandma or someone you trust.
If possible, read in nature while grounding and being very intentional. .

Introduction: She Didn't Just Teach Me—She Transformed Me

This is a book about wisdom.
But not the kind you get from textbooks or degrees.
This is lived wisdom—spirit-tested, storm-approved, blood-bound truth passed from one woman to another with love, with fire, with undeniable grace.

My grandmother was no ordinary woman.
She didn't just raise children—she raised real ones.
She didn't just give advice—she gave codes.
She didn't just talk—she trained.

Her words could clean your soul like fresh river water, and her silence could teach you more than a thousand sermons.

She was elegance and edge.
Prayer and precision.
Softness wrapped in steel.

A light being in the flesh of a woman who had seen too much, felt too much, but never let life break her.

And when I lost my footing, it was her voice that steadied me.
When I questioned my worth, it was her gaze that reminded me.

When the world tried to strip me down to nothing, it was her words that stitched me back together with purpose and power.

This book is a record of that stitching.
A remembering.
A return.

It's not written for applause. It's written for awakening.
It's not written to be trendy. It's written to be true.
It's not for everyone.

But it is for the one ready to stop dimming, stop doubting, and stop abandoning themselves for crumbs when they were born to carry thrones.

You'll hear her voice through every page.
Sometimes she'll whisper. Sometimes she'll roar.
Sometimes she'll remind you who you are, and sometimes she'll remind you who you've never been.
But through it all, she's holding your hand.
Steady. Sacred. Unshaken.

This isn't a self-help book.
It's a soul-remembrance.

If you've ever been made to feel like too much or not enough...

If you've ever been silenced, sidelined, or spiritually gaslit...
If you've ever forgotten who you were because life kept demanding who you had to be...

Let this book bring you back.
Not to the old version of you.
But to the real one.
To the whole one.

To the one Grandma already saw in you—before you even saw it yourself.

Dedication

I dedicate this book to my grandmother—
the first altar I ever knew,
the first warrior I ever watched win battles in silence,
and the first love who never made me question my worth.

You didn't just raise me.
You revealed me.

You didn't just teach me to survive.

You showed me how to stand—with dignity,
with power, with peace that could not be stolen.

You taught me that being soft is not the absence of strength—
It is the mastery of it.

You told me,
I am not a rug. I am not to be walked over.
I am sacred. I am chosen. I am complete.

And I believed you—
because you lived it.

This is for every whisper you gave
when no one was listening.
For every prayer you said that held up my bones.

For every lesson, every look, every moment
you never needed recognition for.

You are the reason I know how to protect my peace,
preserve my light, and return to my own name.

Thank you for being my beginning,
and my guide—even now.

This is your book,
and I am your legacy.
Forever.

"From Her Heart to My Spirit"

"You are not a carpet, and don't you ever act like one."

That was one of the first sentences my grandmother said to me when I was learning how to be "nice." She said, "Kindness is not stupidity, and compassion doesn't mean self-erasure."

My grandmother was no ordinary woman. She wasn't raised with luxuries, but she moved through the world like royalty. She believed in washing not just clothes, but spirits. In her house, dirt wasn't just a sanitation issue—it was a spiritual concern.

"Stay clean," she would say, "because spirits are watching."

Everything she taught me planted seeds. About power. About protection. About not letting people play in your mind or spirit.

This book is my way of passing her legacy forward. Not just for me, but for anyone who needs to hear that you are not too much, not too loud, not too sacred, not too powerful. You are exactly who you're meant to be, and this world better get used to it.
Let these words sit with you. Let her voice echo in your spirit. This is more than a memoir—it's a call to rise.

Chapter 1: I Am Not a Rug

Boundaries, Self-Worth & Refusing to Be Walked Over

"Listen to me, my child… I didn't come all this way, through fire and storms, just for you to let someone drag you like dust on their shoes. You are not a rug. You hear me? You are not a rug."

She said it with that stillness that cut through all my overthinking. She wasn't loud. She didn't raise her voice. But her words? They stood up in the room.

I remember one of the first times I cried in front of her because someone I loved deeply had disrespected me. Again. I had bent backwards, twisted myself into forgiveness, and tried to make excuses for them—because I "loved them," because I didn't want to lose anyone else.

She leaned in, looked me dead in my eyes and said, "You are not a doormat for the emotionally bankrupt. You are not their second chance, their apology dump, or their ego boost. And you surely ain't their punching bag. You're a whole soul with sacred blood in your veins. You better act like it."

She said it with so much certainty that the tears dried up before they could finish falling.

Then she held my hand—the one I always clenched too tight when I was trying to hold everything together—and said:

"Let me teach you something… boundaries are not punishments. They are preservations. You don't set them because you're mean. You set them because you're divine."

I listened, heart still raw. And she kept going.

"They'll call you difficult. They'll say you've changed. Let them. That's their discomfort meeting your divinity. That's their control issues clashing with your sovereignty. Not your problem, never was. You don't need to be liked to be respected. You don't need to be accepted to be aligned."

She told me that love without boundaries isn't love—it's sacrifice.
She told me that peace without truth isn't peace—it's performance.
She told me that I didn't owe anyone anything except the truth of who I am.

"Even if you have nothin' in your hand," she said, "even if the world looks at you and sees loss, I still see power. Power don't come from paper and pearls. It comes from presence. And baby, your presence is heavy. Too heavy to be dragged."

Then she leaned back in her chair, slow and dignified, as if the very air around her was listening too.

"I didn't raise no woman-child to fold every time someone's voice got loud or hands got clever. I raised you to stand, even when standing shakes your knees."

I remember sitting in silence for a moment, not because I didn't believe her—but because the truth was rearranging me.

I had spent, well invested, so much of my life trying not to be "too much," trying to be "good," trying to be easy to love and quick to forgive. But all I had done was lower my worth to fit into places that were never meant to hold me.

"Stop being polite when your spirit is on fire," she said. "Stop trying to fix people who are committed to misunderstanding you. Set the boundary. Shut the door. Reclaim your breath."

She told me that I wasn't supposed to be everyone's "yes."
She reminded me that even the sun takes breaks behind the clouds—and it's still the sun.

That even when I'm quiet, I'm loud in energy. That even when I've lost things, I've gained myself.

"You're not crazy for walking away," she said. "You're wise. You're not cold for choosing peace. You're mature. You're not rude for protecting yourself. You're healed."

"You're not crazy for walking away," she said. "You're wise. You're not cold for choosing peace. You're mature. You're not rude for protecting yourself. You're healed."

Grandma's Closing Word

"Let 'em talk. Let 'em go. Let 'em wonder why you disappeared from their circus. You've got bigger things to do than be anyone's soft landing while they keep throwing bricks. You are not a rug. You are the floor they wish they could walk on, the light they pretend doesn't blind them, the gate they will never pass through again."

Chapter 2: Stay Clean in Spirit and Body

Hygiene as a Sacred Practice

"My baby, stay clean. Not just for looks. For spirit. For power. For the light inside you. You hear me? Dirt invites demons. Cleanliness? That's where the Divine stays."

She always said it like a commandment. And not one of fear—but of reverence.
There was nothing casual about hygiene in my grandmother's house.

Baths weren't rushed. They were rituals.
Clothes weren't just washed. They were blessed.

The body wasn't just something to decorate—it was the temple, the altar, the walking church.

"You ever notice how the streets stay dirty and dark?" she asked one evening as we were folding fresh laundry. "It's not just the trash outside—it's the despair. When people don't feel worthy, they stop washing. And when they stop washing, they attract what mirrors that. Spirits you don't want."

She wasn't judging—she was warning.
I used to think cleanliness was about impressing others. She corrected me quickly.

"It's not to show off your perfume or pretty shirt. It's to align your spirit. When you clean your body, you shake off the energy that tried to stick. The envy. The doubt. The curses they threw at you behind fake smiles. That's what soap is for. That's what water remembers."

She told me to never underestimate a cold rinse in the morning, or a warm bath at night. She told me to scrub my feet not just to soothe them—but to honor the path I walk. To bless my steps. To clear the footprints of those who wished me harm.

"Your hygiene is your shield, your mirror, your protection," she whispered as she washed my hair one evening, pouring warm water slowly so it touched my scalp just right. "You think they don't know that? The ones who want to harm you? That's why they show up with stink attitudes and dirty minds. They been rolling with spirits that haven't bathed in years."

I laughed. But she didn't.

"Laugh if you want, but I've seen what dirt hides. I've seen what mold grows in unwashed spaces—spiritually and otherwise. Keep your house clean. Keep your body clean. And most of all—keep your spirit clean. 'Cause when filth piles up, blessings don't flow, they clog."

It was spiritual hygiene. Always.

"Sprinkle salt near your door. Burn something holy when the air feels heavy. Wipe your mirrors. Wash your underwear like you respect yourself. Your body's not just flesh—it's legacy. So don't just clean it—honor it."

I never forgot those words.

She said people might call you obsessive. Say you're "extra" for bathing twice a day, or for not allowing shoes in your home, or for keeping your towels separated from others. But it was never just about rules.

It was about ritual. It was about setting a frequency in your life that nothing unclean—physically or spiritually—could enter.

"They think we clean to impress?" she'd ask. "We clean to command. To declare to every spirit watching: This house, this body, this life—belongs to the light."

I understood later what she meant. That some people live in chaos not because they want to—but because they stopped believing they deserved beauty, order, and light.

"You are not one of them," she reminded me constantly. "When you wake up and clean yourself, you're saying to the world: 'I remember who I am. I am worthy of care. I am worthy of clarity. I am a vessel of the divine.'"

And when people would show up smelling foul, acting reckless, living in mess, she'd whisper:

"They lost their mirror. Don't let them fog up yours."

Reflection Prompt

Take a moment to ask yourself:
- Have I treated hygiene as sacred, or as an afterthought?
- What clutter—physically or emotionally—am I tolerating in my space, body, or spirit?
- When was the last time I washed not just my body, but my energy?
- Do I clean from obligation or from honor?

Write down 3 sacred hygiene rituals you will commit to—starting today.

Activation Practice: Divine Hygiene Ritual
Morning Water Blessing

Upon waking, speak into your water before washing your face:

"May everything that is not mine be washed away. May I stand clean, inside and out."

Evening Energy Rinse

During your bath or shower, say:

"Every touch, word, and look that did not serve me— be removed now. I return to my essence. I return to my glow."

House Clearing Practice
- Sweep your space while saying: "Only peace may dwell here. Only light may enter."
- Open windows. Light incense, herbs, or simply play soft high-frequency music.
- Sprinkle salt at the door and say: "No evil shall cross this line. My space is clean. My soul is fortified."

Grandma's Closing Word

"My beautiful one… stay clean like your spirit depends on it. Because it does. Don't let no one with unwashed hands touch your destiny. You are the altar. Don't ever let dirt build on something so holy."

Chapter 3: You Are a Magnet

Desire, Attraction, and Not Begging

"Baby girl... stop begging. You are a magnet. You don't chase. You attract. You command. You summon. You draw in. And anything that can't find you? It wasn't meant for you."

That's how she started that lesson. Straight to the soul.

I had just told her how tired I was—from trying so hard to prove I was worth loving. Tired from applying to everything, giving to everyone, being loyal to those who barely showed up for me. My spirit was loud with desperation, and my smile was cracking from the weight of trying.

She pulled me close, wiped the tears before they could fall, and said:

"You are not an application form. You are not a request. You are not a backup plan waiting for approval. You are the magnet. And magnets don't beg. They pull."

She had a way of saying things that made everything stop spinning.

"What you desire is already looking for you," she said. "But you keep blocking it with desperation. That ain't alignment—that's panic."

Then she looked me over like she was reading my energy, not just my face.

"Listen to me... stop knocking on doors that your spirit already told you were closed. Desire what you want, but don't bow to it. You hear me? If you have to crawl to keep it, it was never yours. You want love? Be love. You want peace? Radiate peace. You want abundance? Walk like you already got it."

She reminded me that the most powerful people she knew didn't move fast. They moved sure.
They didn't chase after validation—they anchored in truth.

They didn't scream "choose me"—they chose themselves over and over again.

"When you know your worth," she said, "you stop fighting to be picked. You start picking."
I asked her how to stop feeling like I was behind, like I was lacking.

She smiled and poured me a glass of water.
"Drink that," she said. "Now tell me—did you chase the water, or did you just receive it?"

I blinked.

"That's how your blessings work. You open. You receive. You stay clean, aligned, and available. Stop crowding your spirit with things that are not for you. You ain't ever needed to beg for anything. If you're still breathing, you already got more than enough to get started."

And when I told her I didn't have much—no money, no connections, no idea what my next step was—she didn't flinch.

"You got breath, don't you? You got a heartbeat? You got ears to listen and hands to build? Then you're not empty. You're already full. You just need to remember it."

She taught me that desire was not about lack—it was about alignment. That I could want more and still be whole. That I didn't need to beg for friendship, love, or opportunities. My job was to prepare, position, and protect my field.

"You plant," she said, "and then you water. And then you wait. But you don't scream at the soil to grow. You let the sun and the ancestors do their part. Don't rush the divine."

Reflection Prompt
- Where in my life am I chasing instead of attracting?
- What am I begging for that might actually be draining me?
- What would it look like if I believed I was already worthy, already magnetic?

Write a list of the top 5 things you desire in life. Then beside each, write the version of you who naturally attracts that into her life—not through struggle, but through alignment.

Activation Practice: The Magnetic Self Ritual
Magnetic Mirror Mantra

Look at yourself in the mirror every morning and say aloud:

"I am a magnet. What is mine flows to me effortlessly. I radiate clarity, power, and peace."

Desire Without Desperation

Take 3 minutes a day to breathe deeply and visualize your desires. Then release them to the Divine.

Say:
"I plant these seeds and release control. I walk in alignment, not fear."

Light Calling Ritual

Light a white or gold candle. Sit with it for 7 minutes in silence and whisper:

"All that is meant for me is finding its way to me. I am ready, I am worthy, I am aligned."

Grandma's Closing Word

"Let them look shocked when you stop running after crumbs. Let them feel confused when your back is turned and your boundaries are firm. You are the magnet, not the mule. You were never meant to carry other people's neglect just to feel seen. Your light is enough. Your breath is sacred. You already got what you need. Now act like it."

Chapter 4: When the Chest Feels Heavy

Discernment and Spirit-Led Decisions

"When your chest feels heavy, baby… that's not anxiety. That's your spirit speaking. That's your warning. That's your wisdom knocking. Listen. Before the storm comes, the body already knows."

She used to tap her own chest when she said that, gently, like reminding herself too.

I remember one day when I had a decision to make.
It looked good on paper. Sounded right in conversation. Everybody around me said, "Go for it."
But something in me just… tightened.
A knot. Right in the center of my chest.
I thought I was nervous. She said no.

"That's not nerves. That's knowing. And if you ignore it, you'll regret it. The body speaks before the disaster. But most people only listen after the damage."

I paused.
"That heavy feeling?" she said, "It's your ancestors pulling you back. It's your higher self raising a red flag. And if you push past it just to please people, you're the one who's gonna pay the price."

She was right. Every time I ignored that weight in my chest, that unease in my gut, I paid. Emotionally. Spiritually. Sometimes financially.

"The world trains you to think logic is louder than spirit," she said. "But spirit doesn't shout. Spirit presses. If you feel pressed, baby, pay attention."

She told me stories of her own—times she ignored that feeling and ended up in places, around people, in situations that stole her peace.
She didn't want that for me.

"Don't move just 'cause something looks shiny. You ain't no raccoon. You're not here to chase glitter. You're here to grow in gold. And gold takes knowing."
I asked her, "But what if I'm just afraid? What if I'm sabotaging myself?"

She held my face so tender and said:

"Self-sabotage is when you let fear lead. Discernment is when you let wisdom walk first. Baby, your spirit is wise. Don't confuse its caution for fear. Feel the difference."

Then she taught me how to check myself:
"Close your eyes," she'd say. "Breathe deep. If it still feels heavy after you rest, after you pray, after you breathe—don't do it. That's your no. That's your stop sign."

She taught me to sit with decisions, not sprint into them. To wait a day, a week if I had to. To ask: Is this good for my spirit? Does it make me feel safe? Whole? Empowered? Will my future thank me?
If not—it's a no. No matter how fine it looks. No matter how fast it moves.

"If it costs your peace, it's too expensive. If it weighs your chest, it's not of the light. If you feel dread instead of delight, turn around."

Reflection Prompt
- What was the last decision I made that felt heavy in my chest—but I made it anyway?
- Where do I tend to override my inner knowing to avoid disappointing others?
- What does "peace" feel like in my body? What does "no" feel like?

Write out a list of people, places, or plans that bring peace—and another that bring heaviness. The list won't lie. Your body never does.
Activation Practice: Listening to the Body
Breath Discernment Check
Before any major decision, sit still. Close your eyes. Breathe in for 4 seconds, hold for 4, release for 6. Ask your body:
"Is this mine?"
"Is this right for me?"
"Will this water me or wound me?"

Listen to what rises. Trust it.

Daily Body Scan

At the start and end of each day, pause for 3 minutes and mentally scan your chest, your gut, your back. Ask:

"What feels tight? What feels light? What needs to be released?"

Discernment Candle Practice

Light a blue or white candle. Whisper:
"May I know. May I trust. May I wait when I must. May no heaviness guide me."

Grandma's Closing Word

"Let 'em think you slow. Let 'em call you cautious. That's your power. That's your protection. Fast moves ain't always wise ones. When you feel heavy, pause. When you feel pressed, pray. The spirit always knows. And I ain't raise you to ignore your knowing. Your chest is your compass. Your breath is your guide. Don't ever let the noise outside be louder than your peace inside."

Chapter 5: You Are Your Own Savior

Self-Agency & Ancestral Backup

"My child, no one is coming to save you. Not because you're alone... but because you were never meant to be saved. You were born with the power to rise. And when you forget, we—the ancestors—rise with you. But never forget, you must take the first step."

I'll never forget the way she said it.

I was in one of those low seasons. The kind where the silence in your life feels louder than any noise could ever be. I told her I was tired. Tired of hoping people would show up. Tired of waiting for someone to understand. Tired of being strong, tired of being alone, tired of carrying things that weren't even mine.

She looked at me and said it with that quiet fire that only grandmothers who've survived too much can carry:

"You're tired because you're waiting to be rescued. And I'm here to tell you—stop. No one is coming. Not because you're not worth it, but because they can't. This is your mountain. And you? You are the one chosen to climb it."
I was still.

"You are your own savior," she repeated, "and that's not sad—it's sacred. That's not lonely—it's liberation. Because when you save yourself, no one gets to hold your freedom as ransom."

She told me that people will promise to carry you, to help you, to love you through it. And some will mean it. But most don't have the strength to hold their own pain, let alone yours. That's why you must know who you are before you collapse.

"Don't wait on someone's apology to heal. Don't wait on their help to rise. Don't wait for the world to see your worth to start living like you're divine. Baby, do it now. Because your delay gives power to people who never earned it."

Then she stood up. And when she walked across the room, I swear I saw fire around her feet.

"I've lived through famine. I've walked with holes in my shoes and songs in my soul. I've been abandoned, betrayed, beat down, and still woke up the next day to bless the sun. Why? Because I learned early: I am my own answer."

She reminded me that the blood running through me wasn't ordinary. It was battle-tested. Ancestrally blessed.

"When you take your first step, we take the next ten. When you whisper for help, we roar behind you. But you must move. Don't lay there waiting for light when you are the light."

And when I said, "But I don't know how to fix this,"

She simply said:
"You don't need to know how. You need to know who. And baby—you're her. You are her. The one who breaks the chain. The one who starts the fire. The one who finishes the story differently."

Reflection Prompt
- Where in my life have I been waiting for someone else to fix, change, or rescue me?
- What would shift if I believed, fully, that I am my own answer?
- How would I move differently today if I trusted that the ancestors were walking with me?

Write down three things you are waiting for someone else to do—and declare today how you will begin to do them for yourself.

Activation Practice: The Savior Within
Mirror Command
Each morning, face yourself and say:
"I am not waiting. I am walking. I am not lost—I am led. I am my own liberator."

Ancestral Walk

Go outside barefoot or with grounded intention. Walk slowly. With each step, whisper:

"One step for me. Ten steps with me."

Feel the energy of those who came before you, walking behind you, beside you, within you.
Light + Liberation Candle Ritual
Light a red or gold candle. Speak:
"Every power I gave away, I now call back. I activate the Savior in me. I break the lie that I must wait. I rise now."

Grandma's Closing Word

"Don't you ever wait for the world to clap before you dance. Don't wait for them to approve before you rise. You are not a project for fixing. You are a prophecy unfolding. You've got backup, baby. Every ancestor that walked barefoot so you could fly is still with you. But you—you—must take the first step. Say it with me now: I am not waiting. I am rising."

Chapter 6: Walk Barefoot, Listen to the Wind

Nature as Divine Messenger

"When you don't know what to do, baby... don't talk to people. Go outside. Put your feet in the grass. Let the wind touch your face. Let the earth remember you. That's where the real answers come from. Not from mouths, but from the elements."

That was Grandma's remedy. Every time.

Whenever I felt lost, overwhelmed, uncertain—her advice was simple, ancient, and rooted in something far older than the world's noise.

No phone call.
No scrolling.
No self-blame.

Just: "Get outside. Take your shoes off. Touch something real. The answers are already in motion."

At first, I didn't understand. I thought it was just another way to distract myself.

But Grandma didn't do distractions. She did divine reminders.

"The wind is not just breeze, child—it's breath. When

it blows, it brings whispers. Secrets. Messages from your soul and the ones who came before you. But if you never get quiet, you'll never hear it."

She said the ground speaks too.

"Put your feet on the earth. Let her talk to you. Let her pull the tension from your bones. She's not just dirt—she's a memory bank. A medicine woman. A witness to everything. And when you touch her, she remembers who you are and what you came here for."

I'll never forget the day I finally tried it, after a week of grief, confusion, and constant mental fog. I turned everything off, walked out to the backyard, kicked off my shoes, and stood in the grass.

And just like she said…
My body sighed.
My mind slowed.
And for the first time in days—I heard me again.
I could hear Grandma in my spirit too.

"Don't be ashamed to talk to the wind like it's an old friend. Because it is. Don't feel silly putting your hand in a river and asking it to take your worries. It will. Don't second-guess sitting by a tree with your back against it, telling it your heart. The tree won't betray you like people will."

She taught me that nature wasn't a backdrop—it was a sacred partner.

"Before people, there were the elements. Before religion, there were rivers. Before trauma, there was sun and sky. You've been looking for healing in the wrong places. Go back to the original temple."

She told me that when everything felt like too much, and I didn't want to talk to anyone...

"Don't talk to anyone, talk to everything. The trees. The wind. The moon. They will answer. Not always in words, but in knowing. In peace. In sudden clarity. That's how the divine talks when you listen without your mouth."

Reflection Prompt

- When was the last time I connected with nature without distraction?
- What has the wind, the earth, or the sky been trying to tell me that I've been too busy to hear?
- Where can I create moments each week to unplug and receive from nature?

Write out 3 specific places or ways you can return to nature this week—and commit to one time to walk barefoot, undisturbed, even if only for a few minutes.

Activation Practice: The Elemental Listening Ritual

Barefoot Grounding
Step outside barefoot. Stand still. Say:

"Earth beneath me, remember me. Pull from me all that is not mine. Refill me with strength, stability, and clarity."

Wind Whispering
On a windy day, close your eyes. Feel the breeze.

Speak:
"Blow through me. Carry away confusion. Whisper to me what my spirit has forgotten."
Then stand in silence and let the moment come.

Water Hand Cleansing

Dip your hands in a bowl of water (or a river/ocean if possible). Say:

"Wash away the fog. Reveal my truth. Soften what's hardened in me."

Sunlight Soak
Let sunlight touch your face or chest. Speak softly:

"Shine through me. Melt away fear. Illuminate the path ahead."

Grandma's Closing Word

"You don't need another opinion, my child. You need alignment. And alignment begins with silence. The kind of silence only nature offers. So go barefoot. Talk to the wind. Lay your burdens in the grass. The earth is older than your pain. She knows what to do with it. And remember—when no one else hears you, nature always does. She's been listening since your first breath."

Chapter 7: Your Star Will Burn Them

Spiritual Authority & Chosen Identity

"Let me tell you something once and for all—no one, and I mean no one, can steal your light. If they try to touch your star, it will burn them. You were born marked. Chosen. And chosen ones don't beg to belong. They come to break patterns."

Grandma didn't whisper when she said that. She said it with heat. With certainty. With the kind of conviction only someone who's seen spiritual warfare with her own eyes could carry.

She had sensed it before I did. The tension. The attacks. The jealousy I couldn't explain.

The rooms I'd walk into and feel resistance before I'd even speak.

The "friends" who'd praise me in public but pick at my shine behind closed doors.

"They don't dislike you 'cause you did something wrong," she said. "They dislike you because your presence does something to their unhealed spirit. Your light exposes what they've been hiding from. That ain't your fault. But it is your power."

She was right. And deep down, I always knew it.
Even as a child, I felt different. Not better—but activated. As if I carried a message I hadn't fully remembered yet. And people could sense it too, even if they didn't have the words. Sometimes they loved me for it. Other times, they tried to kill it.

"Don't you ever shrink to make others feel taller," she warned me. "If they want your level, they better rise. You ain't built for bowing. You were born to blaze."

I told her I felt guilty when others felt uncomfortable around me, when they projected envy or criticism. I asked her if I should dim a little—just to keep the peace.

She didn't even let me finish.

"Peace without truth is just quiet oppression. Don't you ever dim, baby. That's how stars die. You're not here to be easy to look at. You're here to lead."

She reminded me that I didn't need titles or degrees to be divine. My identity didn't come from validation. It came from origin.

"You come from a long line of seers, protectors, midwives of the spirit. You didn't choose this path—it chose you. And every time you try to forget, life will remind you. Because your star is coded. It's etched into the sky. Even if they pretend not to see it, it still shines."

She told me people would try to delay me. Distract me. Dismantle my confidence with subtle jabs and spiritual doubt. But my power was not up for negotiation.

"Don't argue with them. Don't prove anything. Just keep walking. Your elevation will silence them before your mouth ever needs to open."

Reflection Prompt

- Where in my life have I dimmed to make others feel comfortable?
- Who am I when I am not apologizing for my power?
- What would happen if I stopped negotiating my worth and started standing in it—fully?

List 5 ways your light has triggered others—and reflect on how you can stop shrinking in response.

Activation Practice: The Star's Authority
Anointed Mirror Affirmation

Each morning, place your hand over your heart and say:

"I am chosen. I am seen. I am not here to fit in—I am here to radiate. My light is not up for debate."

Salt + Fire Star Protection

Sprinkle a line of salt across your doorway. Light a candle (white or red). Say:

"Any force that tries to dull my shine, may it be turned away. My star is protected. My path is clear. I rise with fire."

Silent Walking Meditation

Go for a walk under the stars (or in nature). In your mind, repeat:

"I am marked. I am mighty. My ancestors walk with me."
Feel their power as your cloak.

Grandma's Closing Word

"Let them talk. Let them gossip. Let them glare. You didn't come here to be small. You came here to shift generations. And when they try to steal your shine, remember—you are the flame. They can't touch you without getting burned. Keep rising. Keep glowing. And never forget, child—your star is your stamp. Not even time can erase it."

Chapter 8: Don't Shrink for Nobody

Authenticity vs. Conformity

"I better not ever catch you shrinking, not even a little bit. Not for a man, not for a boss, not for no friend, not even for family. You were born to take up space. So take it. Loud, bold, and fully."

Grandma didn't believe in playing small.
She didn't believe in "toning it down" or "being less intimidating."
She said the world already had enough dimmed lights—what it needed was truth, embodied.

And to her, shrinking was a silent betrayal of the soul.
"Every time you shrink, you send a signal to your spirit that it don't deserve to be seen. That's a lie. Don't you ever lie on your spirit."

I used to shrink without even noticing it.
Sitting quiet in rooms where I had something to say.
Laughing off disrespect just to avoid tension.
Dimming my beauty, my power, my intelligence so no one would feel "less than" around me.

"You better stop that mess," she told me one afternoon while braiding my hair. "You think you're being humble. But what you're doing is hiding. That's not humility, that's self-betrayal."

She said if people were uncomfortable with my light, they had two options:

Put on shades…
Or leave the room.

"You didn't come here to make others comfy. You came here to be yourself—fully, beautifully, radically. That's your job. The rest is their business."

She reminded me that shrinking might feel like protection at first—but in the long run, it becomes a prison. A cage where your greatness suffocates slowly.

"Every time you lower your volume to suit them, you raise their power over you. And one day, you'll forget what you sound like. Don't do that to yourself, baby."
I asked her once, "But what if they leave me?"

She smiled wide and fierce.
"Then let 'em leave. You think your worth is based on who sticks around? Your worth is fixed. It doesn't go up when they love you or down when they don't. You better know who you are when the room claps and when it doesn't."

She taught me that conformity kills creativity. That the world needs the real me—not the edited version, not the watered-down one.

"You ain't here to be a clone. You ain't here to be a good girl or a silent statue. You're here to be a force. So stop apologizing. Start radiating."

Reflection Prompt

- Where do I still shrink myself in order to be accepted, liked, or less "intimidating"?
- What part of me have I hidden that is craving to be free?
- What would my life look like if I let myself be fully seen—even if it made others uncomfortable?

Write a letter to the parts of yourself you've silenced. Then write a declaration of freedom for them.

Activation Practice: Radiance Reclamation
Mirror Expansion Affirmation

Stand tall. Shoulders back. Head high. Say aloud:

"I will not shrink. I will not dim. I will not disappear to soothe someone else's shadow. I take up space, and I do so with love and power."

Candle of Fullness
Light a bright candle (yellow, white, or orange). Stand in front of it and say:

"I ignite every part of me that has been hidden. I call myself back into fullness. I am not too much—I am just right."

Voice Unleashing Exercise
Speak your truth aloud every day—even if just to yourself. Choose one phrase that feels powerful and repeat it with volume and authority.

Try:
"I don't apologize for existing."
"I am here on purpose."
"I don't shrink—I shine."

Grandma's Closing Word
"They'll tell you to be quiet. To settle. To 'just be grateful.' Don't listen. You were not made to blend in. You are the main color, the main voice, the main presence. And if they get uncomfortable, let them sit with it. That's their healing to do. You? You walk tall, head up, chest forward, spirit on fire. Don't shrink for nobody. You hear me? Not ever again."

Chapter 9: They'll Try to Imprint You

Protection from Jealous Spirits
"There are people who won't even know why they hate you. But I do. It's 'cause your spirit walks in like a mirror—and they can't stand what they see. And when they can't copy you, they'll try to crush you. Don't let them."

Grandma saw it before I did.
The way people would linger too long around me… not out of admiration, but calculation.
The way they'd compliment me with their mouth, but curse me with their eyes.

The way they'd study me, borrow from me, mimic me—and then turn on me the moment I stood tall in something they couldn't reach.

"They'll try to imprint their fears, their bitterness, their envy onto you," she warned. "They'll speak subtle curses in jokes, plant seeds of doubt in conversations, smile while stripping your confidence piece by piece. That's not love, baby. That's spiritual theft."

I used to take it personally.
I thought maybe if I was kinder, softer, smaller—they'd like me.

But Grandma said:
"You can't please a jealous spirit. You can only protect yourself from it."

She taught me how to feel the shift in a room. How to see past the sweet words and feel the vibration.
She told me that when a person's presence makes you feel unsure of yourself—it's not you. It's them. It's their imprint trying to override your truth.

"Some people don't come into your life to support you," she said. "They come to study your blueprint, hijack your voice, and then try to gaslight you into believing you were never powerful in the first place."

That lesson was hard—but it saved my life.
"They'll say you're selfish when you protect your energy. They'll say you're mean when you stop giving them your secrets. They'll say you're cold when you stop letting them feed off your warmth. Let them talk. Protect yourself anyway."

She told me to be watchful—not paranoid, but present.

"Don't walk around suspicious of everybody," she said. "But don't ignore your gut when it whispers. Especially when it whispers about someone you 'love.' Envy doesn't always come from strangers—it often comes from those who sit closest."

Then she taught me how to spiritually shield myself:

"Start your day with prayer and fire. Anoint your head, your feet, your words. Speak your boundaries before you leave your house. And never forget—you don't need to let people into your world just 'cause they smile. Smiles lie. Vibes don't."

Reflection Prompt

- Who in my life drains me but disguises it as friendship or concern?
- Where have I allowed others to place their fears and jealousy onto me?
- What would my energy look like if I stopped letting others imprint on me?

List five names or energies you need to spiritually distance from. Then write an intention to clear and reclaim your space.

Activation Practice: Aura Protection Ritual
Verbal Boundary Setting (Every Morning)
Before you step out or go online, speak aloud:

"My energy is mine. My joy is mine. My ideas are mine. No one may enter my field unless they come with light and truth."

Salt and Mirror Shielding

Place a small mirror facing outward near your front door and sprinkle salt beneath it.

Say:
"Any spirit that brings envy or harm shall see themselves and turn back."

Candle + Cloak Invocation
Light a white candle and wrap yourself in a scarf, shawl, or garment with intention.

Say:
"I cloak myself in divine light. No imprint but my own shall live here. I reject projections, I return to essence."

Grandma's Closing Word
"You don't owe anyone access to your spirit. Not a friend, not a lover, not a cousin, not a coworker. This is your sanctuary. Don't let them write on your walls. Keep your field clean. Keep your light pure. And when they come masked as love, but leave your heart heavy—cut the cord. That ain't love, that's leeching. And you're not here to be drained. You're here to shine, live, and *rise above it all."

Chapter 10: Take a Break, Then Fly

Avoiding Burnout and Rest as Rebellion

"The world will drain you dry if you let it. People will pull and pull until there's nothin' left. So don't wait for permission, baby. When your soul says rest—you rest. When it says stop—you stop. Then? You fly."

That's how she said it.
No apology. No guilt. No disclaimers.
Because Grandma didn't believe in hustle culture.
She believed in wholeness.

She watched me once, spiraling. Saying yes to everyone. Taking every call. Pushing through every headache. Smiling when I wanted to scream. Showing up when I should've been sitting down.

She didn't even raise her voice.

She just said:

"You gon' run yourself into the ground. And baby, let me tell you something—that ground don't give you no badge for being broken."

I sat down real quiet. Tired. Overworked. Trying to prove myself to people who never even asked for me to win—they just expected me to give.

"They don't care how much you do," she said. "They just know you will do it. Until one day, you stop. And the day you stop? That's when you finally start living."

She wasn't saying don't work hard. She worked her whole life.

But she worked in alignment—not in chains.

"You gotta know when to lay down your tools. Know when to pull back your power. Ain't nobody gonna protect your energy but you. So you better treat it like it's sacred. Because it is."

She told me rest wasn't laziness. Rest was strategy.

That too many people were worn out, not because life was too hard—but because they were too afraid to stop. Afraid someone might replace them. Outshine them. Or forget them.

"Let 'em forget," she said. "While they chase the crowd, you recover your crown. You don't need to be seen every minute to still be powerful. Some of your growth will happen in silence—and that's exactly how it should be."

She even told me that rest was warfare. A kind of rebellion against systems that taught us we're only worthy if we're producing, performing, and pleasing others.

"Every time you rest, you say: I am not a machine. I am divine. Every time you rest, you say: My worth ain't tied to how much I can endure. Every time you rest, you win."

Then she smiled like she knew I was finally getting it. "Don't just rest when you break down. Rest so you don't have to. That's the difference between survival and sovereignty. Choose sovereignty."

Reflection Prompt

- Where am I pushing myself to prove something—to others or to myself?
- What part of me believes I have to earn rest?
- When was the last time I rested with no guilt, no shame, no explanation?

Write down 3 things you need to pause or say "not right now" to. Then write 3 things you'll do to nourish yourself instead.

Activation Practice: Sacred Rest Ritual
Candle of Permission
Light a calming candle (lavender, blue, or white). Speak:

"I give myself permission to rest. I honor my body. I refill my soul. I choose peace without guilt."

The 20-Minute Reset
Set a timer. Turn off all screens. Lay down with hand on heart. Breathe in this mantra:

"I am safe. I am whole. I am allowed to rest."

Feather Writing Practice
Write a letter to your inner child or future self.

Start with:
"You don't have to earn your rest. I love you enough to stop. I will not break myself to prove I'm worthy."

Grandma's Closing Word

"You don't always have to fight. Sometimes the greatest fight is saying no. Saying stop. Saying not today. And when you finally lay your burdens down and take your rest, baby, that's when your wings come in. That's when you stop walking—and you fly. So rest, my love. Not because you're weak, but because you're wise. They'll run themselves ragged. But you? You gon' float."

Chapter 11: Fast When It's Good Too

Gratitude as a Lifestyle

"Don't just fast when things go wrong. Fast when it's good too. That's how you show the Divine you're not just in it for rescue—you're in it for relationship."

She said that with her eyes closed, holding her cup of warm herbal tea, sun hitting her skin. She wasn't rushing. She wasn't begging.

She was in tune.

I remember asking her why she still fasted and prayed even when everything seemed to be going well.

Her bills were paid. Her body was healthy. Peace was in the house.
So why sacrifice food? Why wake up before the sun?
She smiled.

"Because I'm not only talking to God when I'm in a storm. I'm building. I'm honoring. I'm saying thank you. Not just with my words—but with my will."

She told me that most people only know how to pray from pain.
They only know how to fast when everything's falling apart.

But that kind of devotion is transactional.
What she wanted to teach me was relational.

"Fasting when life is good keeps you humble. Keeps you connected. It reminds you that blessings don't mean you stop listening. In fact, that's when you should listen even closer."

She said fasting in joy was a way of planting seeds for the future—preparing for storms you didn't even see coming yet, strengthening your spiritual immunity before the test arrived.

"The ones who fast only in crisis stay in crisis. The ones who fast with gratitude build spiritual wealth. And baby, spiritual wealth will carry you when money, people, and plans fall through."

She wasn't just talking about food.

"Sometimes fasting means turning off the noise. Logging out. Not spending. Not gossiping. Not over-explaining yourself. It means choosing stillness so you can actually hear what's sacred."

She told me the Divine keeps records—not just of what you ask for, but when you pause to say thank you with your actions.

"It's easy to praise when you're in pain and you want

something. But who are you when life is good? Do you still show up in reverence?"

I didn't have an answer at first. But I do now.

"Be the one who gives thanks not just with your mouth—but with your schedule. With your focus. With your discipline. That's how blessings multiply."

Reflection Prompt

- Do I only turn to prayer, fasting, or sacred practices when I'm in crisis?
- How can I begin building a relationship with Spirit based on devotion, not desperation?
- What would it look like to fast or pause as an act of love instead of need?

List three things you can temporarily release—even during times of joy—to realign with gratitude.

Activation Practice: Gratitude Fast Ritual
Morning Gratitude Fast (Non-Food)

Choose one thing you normally indulge in—music, social media, sweets, or excess talk—and release it for the day. In its place, repeat:

"I'm not empty—I'm being filled. I'm not lacking—I'm listening."

Silent Praise Pause

Find 5 minutes in your day to sit still and say nothing. Place your hands on your lap and say in your heart:

"Thank you, thank you, thank you—for what I see, and what I don't yet understand."

Candle + Whisper Offering

Light a candle and whisper 10 things you're grateful for that have nothing to do with material success.

Let each whisper be an offering.

Grandma's Closing Word

"The ones who fast in pain are searching. But the ones who fast in peace? They're anchoring. Don't just come to the Divine when you're in need. Come when you're full too. Come with your joy. Come with your peace. That's how you show Spirit you're not here just to survive—but to serve, to grow, to rise. That's what separates the vessels from the visitors. And baby, you? You're a vessel. So honor it like one."

Silent Praise Pause (Let's try this again)

Find 5 minutes in your day to sit still and say nothing. Place your hands on your lap and say in your heart:

"Thank you, thank you, thank you—for what I see, and what I don't yet understand."

Candle + Whisper Offering

Light a candle and whisper 10 things you're grateful for that have nothing to do with material success.

Let each whisper be an offering.

Grandma's Closing Word

"The ones who fast in pain are searching. But the ones who fast in peace? They're anchoring. Don't just come to the Divine when you're in need. Come when you're full too. Come with your joy. Come with your peace. That's how you show Spirit you're not here just to survive—but to serve, to grow, to rise. That's what separates the vessels from the visitors. And baby, you? You're a vessel. So honor it like one."

Chapter 12: When They Can't Empathize, Walk Like Royalty

Inner Nobility in the Face of Rejection

"When the world turns cold, you don't shrink—you straighten your back. You fix your crown and walk through it like royalty. Because you are. And don't you ever forget it just 'cause they did."

Grandma said it after I came to her heartbroken, disappointed by how some people just... didn't care.
I had opened up, shared my truth, my pain, and instead of care, I got silence. Dismissal. Indifference.

They changed the subject.
Some got uncomfortable.
Others just... disappeared.

"Don't expect empathy from those who ain't done their own healing," she said. "You'll bleed out waiting for compassion from people still pretending they don't hurt."

I told her it made me feel invisible, worthless.
Like maybe my pain was too much.
Like maybe I was too much.
She looked at me with that fire in her eyes—the same fire I saw when she walked into a room like it

belonged to her no matter who was there.

"No, baby. You're not too much. They're too small. And just 'cause they don't see the value doesn't mean you don't carry it. You're gold. And gold doesn't apologize when plastic pretends not to see it."

She taught me that people's inability to empathize had nothing to do with me—and everything to do with their emotional poverty.

"They'll twist it and say you're dramatic. That you need attention. No, you need respect. And if they can't give it, don't argue. Don't cry. Don't explain. Just walk—like the crown on your head is real. Because it is."

She said that when people don't understand your pain, they'll try to downplay it, dismiss it, or ignore it altogether.

And that's okay.

"You're not here to be understood by everyone. You're here to understand yourself. You're not here to be held by everyone. You're here to hold your worth."

Then she said something that still echoes in my spirit today:

"There's a difference between being rejected and being redirected. When they can't hold space for your truth, Spirit will send someone who can. Until then, hold space for yourself. And do it like royalty."

She reminded me of who I was when I forgot.
"Royalty ain't just crowns and silk. Royalty is self-respect. Dignity. Walking away with your head high even when your heart's hurting. Royalty is knowing that the ones who can't see you ain't worthy of your light anyway."

Reflection Prompt

- Where in my life have I allowed rejection to shrink me?
- Who have I begged for understanding when what I really needed was distance?
- How would I walk, speak, and carry myself if I remembered that I am royal in spirit?

Write a letter of release to anyone who made you feel small for simply expressing your truth. Then write a declaration to yourself of how you will walk going forward.

Activation Practice: Royal Walk of Return
Mirror Throne Affirmation
Stand in front of a mirror. Look yourself in the eye and say:

"Their rejection is not my reflection. I am worthy. I am royal. I walk with dignity even when they cannot see my crown."

Walk of the Ancestors

Take a walk, even if just across a room. Each step, whisper:

"I walk for me. I walk for her. I walk for all who had to swallow their pain in silence. I walk like royalty—seen or not."

Candle + Drape Ritual

Light a white or gold candle. Place a cloth, shawl, or scarf around your shoulders. Sit or stand and say:

"I cloak myself in remembrance. I honor my story even when others do not. My throne is internal. My crown is divine. And I rise, every time."

Grandma's Closing Word

"The ones who can't hold your truth will try to shrink it. Don't let them. Your pain is not a performance—it's a part of your becoming. And when they can't see you, don't beg. Don't bend. Just walk—like your ancestors taught you. Like I taught you. Like your soul remembers. Because royalty don't beg to be seen. Royalty shines, no matter who's watching."

Chapter 13: Mind Your Own Million

Discipline, Focus, and Financial Power

"If you paid for something—focus on it. Don't play. Don't get distracted. You didn't hand over your money to go scrolling or chatting. You handed it over to build. Now act like it."

Grandma was never loud when she said things like that.
But her words? They didn't need to shout. They landed.

She believed that your money, your time, and your attention were holy. And you don't waste holy things.

"The people who win in life ain't always the smartest or the richest. They're the ones who focus. The ones who stay on task. The ones who mind their business like it's a million-dollar check waiting to be cashed."

She didn't play about discipline.

When I was tempted to procrastinate or jump into someone else's drama, she'd gently ask me:

"Is this gonna pay you? Will this feed your children? Will this grow your business? Will this build your peace? If the answer is no, then why are you giving it your precious energy?"

She told me to mind my mind. Guard my attention. That every second I spent pouring into distractions was a second stolen from my destiny.

"You don't have time to entertain low-frequency people who only come around to drain you. You don't have time to babysit adults who refuse to grow. And you sure don't have time to explain your vision to folks who ain't got vision of their own."

And when I started investing in myself—books, courses, skills—she reminded me:

"You better show up for what you paid for. Go to bed thinking about what you're learning. Wake up ready to apply it. That's how you turn knowledge into wealth."

She taught me that wealth starts in the mind before it ever shows up in the bank.

"Discipline is currency. Focus is investment. And consistency? That's your compound interest."

She didn't need spreadsheets or business degrees to teach financial power.

She lived it.
She saved in silence. Built in peace. Planned without making announcements.

"Don't share your every move," she said. "Let your life speak for itself. Let your fruit tell the story. You don't need followers—you need foundation."

Reflection Prompt

- What is stealing my attention and costing me my future?
- What have I paid for—emotionally, spiritually, or financially—that I haven't shown up for with full commitment?
- Where do I need to tighten my focus and guard my vision?

List 3 financial, spiritual, or personal investments you've made—and how you can recommit to honoring them this week.

Activation Practice: Millionaire Mindset Ritual
Mirror Declaration
Stand in front of a mirror and say aloud:

"I am focused. I am disciplined. I mind my mind and my money. I am building legacy. My life multiplies."

Money Discipline Candle

Light a green or gold candle. With clear intention, say:

"Every dollar I invest (spend) comes back with purpose. Every task I complete builds my future. I do not chase—I create."

Focus Journal Practice

Each morning, write down:

1. What am I building today?
2. What distractions must I say no to?
3. What will my future self thank me for tonight?

Grandma's Closing Word

"The reason they stay broke in spirit and in bank is 'cause they too busy watching everybody else's life. But you? You're different. You were born to mind your business like your life depends on it—'cause it does. You got a million in you, baby. In ideas. In grace. In power. So act like it. Mind your own million. And let the world wonder how you did it in silence."

Chapter 14: You Are the Altar

Stop Searching Outside of Yourself

"They got you running around building altars, lighting candles, placing statues, and bowing before everything and everyone—when the whole time, you didn't realize: You are the altar. You are the sacred space you've been searching for."

That's what Grandma told me the day I asked her how to build a stronger spiritual practice.

I had seen people with elaborate setups—tables full of tools, veves drawn on the floor, statues lining the walls. I admired it.

But Grandma?

She leaned in, placed her hand on my heart, and said:

"Don't get it twisted. The veve is powerful. The candle is a tool. But none of it means anything if you forget where the real power lives. Right here. Inside you."

She wasn't saying to throw away sacred traditions. She was saying: don't idolize the tool over the temple.

"You can go halfway across the world looking for magic, but if you're ignoring the altar that breathes, you're still empty. You've got holy fire in your bones, child. You don't need to perform it. You just need to remember it."

I asked her how I could "activate" my altar, and she gave me that knowing smile, that deep-rooted, ancient grin that said, you already know.

"You activate it every time you speak truth. Every time you trust your intuition. Every time you say no and mean it. Every time you rest. Every time you honor your peace. That's your altar in motion."

She said people would try to distract you with rituals and rules so you'd forget the truth: you don't need to earn divinity—it's your inheritance.

"They'll tell you to look up to the sky, burn this, chant that, follow this priest, that prophet. But the moment you start outsourcing your power, you start leaking your light. It's okay to get guidance, but never give away your center."

She told me to stop asking for signs from everyone else when I hadn't even sat in silence to hear my own soul.

"You are the sign. You are the portal. You are the

prayer your ancestors planted. Why do you keep looking for what's already living in you?"

Then she looked me straight in the eye and said:

"The altar is not on a shelf, baby. The altar is you. So clean your spirit. Respect your body. Keep your word. Speak your truth. Honor your calling. That's sacred living."

Reflection Prompt

- Where in my life am I seeking power outside of myself when I could be activating it within?
- What sacred practices do I engage in without connecting back to my own heart?
- How can I begin honoring my body, mind, and spirit as the temple they are?

Write a love letter to yourself as if you are the sacred altar. Begin with: "Dear Divine Within..."

Activation Practice: Embodying the Living Altar

Candle + Mirror Altar Activation

Light a white candle. Stand before a mirror and place your hand over your heart. Say:

"I am the altar. I carry the sacred fire. I walk in truth. I rise in holiness. Nothing outside of me defines me."

Salt + Oil Body Anointing

Mix a small pinch of salt with oil (coconut, olive, or sacred oil). Rub on your wrists, forehead, and feet.

Say:
"Every step I take is blessed. Every move I make is sacred. I cleanse and crown myself in power."

Altar Breathwork

Sit in stillness. Inhale for 4, hold for 4, exhale for 8. With each breath, say inwardly:

"I am. I am sacred. I am home."

Grandma's Closing Word

"Don't let them confuse you. Don't let them trick you into thinking your power lives in a statue, in a title, in a man, in a ceremony. Those things can guide—but they cannot give you what you already are. You are the altar. You are the blessing. You are the fire. Stand in it. And never again doubt where the true sacred lives—within you."

Chapter 15: Never Sabotage Yourself

The Sacredness of Self-Trust

"Don't you dare betray yourself trying to please this world. There's no reward in that. No blessing. The biggest sin you could ever commit is turning against your own knowing. So promise me—never sabotage yourself again."

That's what Grandma said the day I admitted I had done something I knew wasn't right for me—just to keep the peace.

I ignored the signs.
I shut down my voice.
I knew I was abandoning myself, but I did it anyway.
She didn't yell.
She didn't judge.

She just looked at me with a quiet sorrow and said:

"You knew better. And baby, when you know better and you go against it—that's self-sabotage. That's spiritual betrayal. That's how cracks form in your foundation."

She told me most people sabotage themselves not because they're weak—but because they're afraid.

"Afraid to shine. Afraid to be alone. Afraid to disappoint. Afraid to say no. Afraid to be misunderstood. But let me tell you something, my love: no fear is worth losing yourself for."

She said the betrayal that hurts the most isn't what someone else does to you.
It's what you do to yourself when you silence your spirit.

"The moment you feel the resistance, the discomfort, the little tug in your belly—that's your warning. And when you push past it to please someone else, you cut your own wings."

She wasn't saying life wouldn't get messy.
She was saying: don't keep choosing the mess when you already have the map out of it.

"You were born with inner truth. Inner compass. You sabotage yourself every time you pretend not to feel what you feel. Every time you say 'yes' when your spirit screams 'no.' That's not kindness—that's self-erasure."

She told me that trusting myself was not selfish.
It was sacred.
It was the highest form of worship.

"The Divine gave you intuition for a reason. You think God would give you a compass and want you to ignore it? Stop looking for answers in people's eyes. They don't live in your skin. Trust yourself."

And when I asked her how to forgive myself for the times I'd gone against my knowing, she said:

"Start by telling the truth. Then make a promise. A holy one. 'I will not betray myself again.' And every time you're tempted to repeat the pattern, stop and remember—that your future depends on how honest you are with yourself now."

Reflection Prompt

- Where have I betrayed myself in order to please others or avoid conflict?
- What pattern of self-sabotage am I ready to release?
- How can I rebuild a sacred trust with myself, starting today?

Write a forgiveness letter to yourself. Begin with:

"I see where I hurt you by not listening…"

Activation Practice: Self-Trust Ceremony
Mirror Truth Invocation

Stand in front of a mirror. Look deeply into your own eyes and say:

"I trust myself. I honor my knowing. I will not betray my spirit again. I am safe in my own truth."

Anointing of Inner Agreement

Mix a small amount of oil (your choice) with a drop of warm water. Place it gently over your heart and say:

"I seal my heart with clarity. I choose me. I walk in truth."

Sacred Vow Journal Entry

Write the following in your journal:

"I vow to stop self-sabotaging. I vow to trust my first mind. I vow to believe that my truth is enough. And I vow to forgive myself for every time I didn't know how."

Grandma's Closing Word

"You're not crazy. You were just taught to ignore your truth to survive. But you don't have to live like that anymore. You are not a sacrifice. You are a sanctuary. So guard yourself like one. And if ever you forget again, come back here—where your truth lives. I'll be waiting."

Chapter 16: Your Light Triggers Them

Energetic Boundaries and Awareness

"You didn't do anything wrong. You just walked in glowing. That's it. That's all it took. Your light reminded them of the darkness they're still hiding from. And instead of doing their healing—they attacked yours."

That's what Grandma said the day I asked her, "Why does it feel like people don't like me even when I've done nothing to them?"

She didn't hesitate.

"Because your energy speaks before your mouth ever opens. And some people feel convicted just being in the same room with you. It's not hate—it's discomfort. You carry a frequency they don't know how to hold."

She reminded me that my light wasn't just beauty—it was truth.
And truth doesn't always feel good to people who live in denial.

"They see your glow and feel their own dust. They see your peace and remember their own chaos. It ain't personal, but it is spiritual. And the moment you accept that, the freer you'll be."

She said to stop asking why and start protecting. Not just physically—but energetically.

"You think boundaries are just about saying 'no' with your mouth? No, baby. Boundaries start with the energy you carry. With who you allow into your space. With how long you let them linger. With how much access you give to people who haven't earned your frequency."

She taught me that not everyone could handle the real me.
Not because I was too much—but because they were too unready.

"You don't have to dim just because they cover their eyes. Let them squint. Let them adjust. Or let them leave. But you? You don't shrink."

I told her it still hurt, even if I understood it.

"Of course it hurts," she said. "You want to be loved. You want to be celebrated. But remember this—being triggered is not the same as being attacked. It's their internal storm. Don't become the thunder they're afraid of. Become the sky."

She said some people will try to get close just to

extinguish the very light they were drawn to.
They'll praise you publicly and poison you privately.
That's why awareness matters.

"Learn to feel it. That little pull in your gut when they smile too long, compliment too hard, or hover in your glow without ever watering it. That's your sign. Energy never lies."

Reflection Prompt

- Where have I ignored energetic tension because I wanted to be liked?
- Who in my life triggers a sense of unease—even if they seem kind?
- How can I create energetic boundaries without guilt?

Write down five energetic truths you've been avoiding—and what you need to do to protect your light moving forward.

Activation Practice: Light Armor Ritual
Protection Flame Prayer

Light a white or gold candle. Place your hands over your heart and say:

"My light is sacred. My energy is mine. I am not responsible for the healing others refuse to do. I protect my spirit in love and truth."

Salt Circle Reset

Sprinkle salt in a circle around a mirror or doorway. Say:

"Only those who come with honor and love may pass. My light repels all falsehood."

Aura Bubble Meditation

Close your eyes. Imagine a radiant light wrapping around your body.

Breathe in and say:
"I am surrounded by truth."

Breathe out and say:
"Only love may enter."

Repeat for 3-5 minutes.

Grandma's Closing Word

"Your light is loud, even in silence. And some folks just ain't ready for that kind of volume. That's not your burden to carry. You are not here to convince anyone of your worth. You are here to be it. So protect your glow. Tend to it like it's fire from heaven. Because, baby—it is."

Chapter 17: The Real Battle is Psychological

Staying Rooted in Truth

"They don't have to hit you to break you. All they gotta do is get in your head. That's the battlefield now. It's not fists—it's fear. Not chains—it's confusion. Guard your mind like it's the last key you got left. 'Cause in this world, it just might be."

That's what Grandma told me after I spent days second-guessing myself, replaying conversations, wondering if I was "too sensitive" or "overthinking."

She leaned in close and said:

"You're not crazy. You're under attack. And the worst part is—they do it so subtly, you start doubting yourself instead of them. That's how they win."

She explained that psychological warfare is one of the oldest tricks in the book—especially against the gifted, the different, the chosen.

"They'll twist your truth. Make you question your memory. Dismiss your feelings. Mock your intuition. And if you ain't grounded, you'll start gaslighting yourself."

I nodded slowly, realizing how many times I had done

exactly that.
Watered myself down.

Laughed off violations.
Tried to make myself "easier to love."

"That's the trap," she said. "They plant doubt like it's a seed. And if you don't pull it fast, it grows into silence. That silence becomes shame. And shame? Shame will have you locked in a cage you never agreed to be in."

She taught me that this battle wasn't about who was louder.

It was about who stayed rooted.

"You don't win by arguing. You win by remembering. Remember who you are. What you've seen. What you felt. What your spirit told you. They'll try to shake it loose—but truth has roots. And roots don't run."

I asked her how to stay grounded when the whole world seems to be spinning with manipulation, projection, and mental games.

She said:
"Create anchors. Daily. Repetitive. Sacred. Speak truth into your water. Touch the earth. Write your

own name with love. Keep your rituals tight. 'Cause they will come for your mind first. And if they get that? They don't even need chains—they got your soul."

She told me the most powerful resistance wasn't loud—it was clarity.
Knowing who you are, even when they try to convince you otherwise.

Reflection Prompt

- What thoughts do I carry that were planted by someone else's fear, envy, or control?
- How often do I question myself because someone else questioned me first?
- What truths do I need to return to in order to take back my mind?

Write out a declaration of the truths that keep you grounded—even when the noise is loud.

Activation Practice: Mind Armor Ritual
Truth-Tapping Affirmation

Tap gently on your forehead, heart, and gut while repeating:

"My thoughts are mine. My spirit is whole. My truth cannot be stolen."

Cleansing Word Repetition

Write the following truth 10 times in your journal:

"I trust what I saw. I trust what I felt. I do not need their permission to believe in myself."

Mind Gate Candle Ritual

Light a dark blue or white candle and whisper:

"I close every mental door they tried to sneak through. I reclaim my thoughts. I block their influence. My mind is mine. And only light may live here."

Grandma's Closing Word

"They'll come soft. With smiles. With flattery. With subtle jabs dressed as advice. But you'll feel it. That little tug in your spirit? That's your alarm. Don't ignore it. You ain't crazy, baby—you're clear. And clarity is the greatest resistance in a world built on confusion. Protect it. Nurture it. Stand on it. Because when the mind is fortified? You win the battle before it even begins."

Chapter 18: Don't Fight Back Unless It's Personal

Strategic Defense

"You don't have to swing at everything that moves. Not every battle deserves your breath. But when they make it personal—when they come for what's yours, who's yours, or try to snatch your soul—you finish it. Quick. Clean. And with truth."

That's how Grandma said it. Calm, collected, but fire behind her eyes.

She wasn't a messy woman.
She didn't believe in drama.
She believed in strategy.
She believed in conserving your power until it mattered.

And when it mattered—you showed up as the storm.

"You ain't got to throw hands or curse 'em out every time they run their mouth. Let fools talk. Most of them just hoping you'll waste your shine proving you're right. And every minute you spend reacting to nonsense? That's light lost. Power leaked. Focus stolen."

I told her about a situation where someone had been poking, provoking, baiting me into reacting.

I wanted to clap back.
I wanted to expose them.
I wanted to burn the whole thing down.

She leaned in and said:

"Don't give them a war they don't deserve. That's what they want. They want your peace. Your energy. Your time. And the more you fight the small stuff, the more you miss the bigger prize."

But then she paused and added:

"Now… if they ever cross the line—if they put their hands on you, if they come for your child, your home, your life, your legacy—you end that. You fight with light, but you fight with precision. You don't scream—you strike. You don't flail—you focus."

She reminded me that defending myself doesn't make me angry, bitter, or wrong.

It makes me sovereign.

"They want you defenseless. That's why they paint protectors as 'aggressive.' That's why they label boundaries as 'mean.' But don't you fall for that. You were born to be kind, not conquered."

She said the real wisdom was in knowing when to walk—and when to war.

"Some things deserve silence. Some things deserve surrender. But others? They deserve a sacred stand. That's how you honor yourself. That's how you teach the world who not to play with."

Reflection Prompt

- Where have I been giving energy to unnecessary battles that do not serve my peace?
- What is worth defending in my life—and where must I take a stronger stand?
- What would it look like to protect myself with wisdom instead of reaction?

List three areas where you can withdraw your energy—and one where you must reclaim it now.
Activation Practice: Sacred Warrior Ritual

Mirror Stand Affirmation

Stand tall, feet grounded. Look yourself in the eyes and say:

"I do not fight everything. But when I fight, I do not lose. I protect what is mine. I walk in power, not panic. I am strategic, sovereign, and sacred."

Candle + Threshold Defense
Light a red or white candle. Place a small bowl of water near it.

Say:

"When the battle is mine, I rise with fire. When it is not, I sit in peace. I will not waste my light, but I will defend it."

Ancestral Defense Prayer

Close your eyes and speak:

"Ancestors who walk with me—shield what is mine. Warn me before harm arrives. Fight beside me when I must stand. Give me the wisdom to know the difference."

Grandma's Closing Word

"You ain't gotta fight every fool in the room. That's exhaustion, not evolution. Let the petty pass. Let the noise fade. But if they come for your soul, your family, your gifts, your peace—you show them who they're dealing with. You are not weak. You are not passive. You are strategic. And when the sacred is threatened? You do not lose."

Chapter 19: Keep Track and Stay in the Light

Spiritual Journaling & Recall

"Write it down. Don't trust your memory with everything. Especially not spiritual things. Keep track. 'Cause when the darkness tries to twist the truth—you'll have receipts. And those receipts will save your mind."

That's what Grandma said when she handed me my first journal.

It wasn't fancy. Just a worn little notebook with soft pages and power folded between every line.

"You think you'll remember all the signs, all the dreams, all the warnings, all the blessings? You won't. And that's how confusion creeps in. One forgetful day at a time."

She wasn't being dramatic. She was wise.
She taught me that memory is holy—but it's also fragile. And if I didn't anchor my experiences in writing, I'd lose track of patterns, prayers, answers, attacks, and breakthroughs.

"You don't just journal for emotions," she said. "You journal for clarity. For documentation. For proof.

'Cause when doubt comes knocking—you better have something sacred to open."

She showed me how to write down more than just feelings.

She said:
- Write down what woke you up in the middle of the night.
- Write the dream that felt too real to ignore.
- Write what someone said that shook your spirit.
- Write what you felt when you walked into a room.
- Write the name that came to you out of nowhere.

"The spirit speaks in layers," she said. "But if you don't write it, you'll miss the connection. What seemed random last week might be the missing piece next month."

She told me journaling was a spiritual weapon, a way of keeping your mind clean and your journey mapped.

"They'll try to confuse you later. Make you question what you saw, what you felt, what you knew. But your journal don't lie. Your spirit remembers. You just have to give it space to speak."

She also said to write down the wins. The breakthroughs. The good days. The tiny victories.

"'Cause the enemy don't just attack you through pain—he attacks you through forgetting. And when you forget how far you've come, you start acting like you never moved."

Reflection Prompt

- Where have I allowed forgetfulness to weaken my faith or confidence?
- What moments, signs, or spiritual downloads have I ignored or forgotten that I need to reclaim?
- How can I make journaling part of my spiritual protection and growth?

List three recent events, dreams, or feelings that deserve to be written down—then do it, with full presence.

Activation Practice: Journal as Shield
Journal Invocation

Before writing, place your hand over the page and say:

"This is my record. This is my light. No confusion can live where clarity is kept."

Writing by Fire

Light a candle before journaling, even if just for 5 minutes. As you write, imagine the flame sealing the truth into your timeline.

Spirit-Recall Breathwork

Before bed, breathe deeply and ask your spirit:

"What do I need to remember?"

Write down whatever comes—no matter how strange, subtle, or symbolic.

Grandma's Closing Word

"They'll try to make you forget. Not just your pain—but your power. Not just your triggers—but your triumphs. So keep track, baby. Write it all. Protect your mind from erasure. You don't have to remember everything in the moment—but your journal will. And when the lies come loud? Your pages will speak louder."

Chapter 20: You Are Already Complete

No Need for External Validation

"You came here whole. You don't need fixing, saving, or someone to clap for you to be worthy. You were complete the day you were born. Don't let the world convince you otherwise just because they can't see it."

That's what Grandma said one day when I was chasing validation like it was oxygen.

Trying to prove myself.
Waiting for approval.

Craving acknowledgment from people who barely knew themselves.

"You want someone to crown you, baby—but you don't need a crown to be royal. You just need to remember."

She saw how much I shrank after silence.
How much I questioned myself when I didn't get a response.

When they didn't clap.
When they didn't text back.
When they didn't say "good job."

"You're not crazy for wanting connection," she said.

"But don't confuse attention with alignment. Don't confuse silence with shame. And don't confuse rejection with a reflection of your worth."

She told me the world profits off insecurity.
That whole systems are built on making you believe you need something external to be whole—more followers, more praise, more love, more affirmation.

"But you? You are the affirmation. You are the evidence. You are the answer."

She reminded me that real completion doesn't mean perfection.
It means enough-ness.

"You're not a half waiting to be found. You're a force waiting to remember."

She told me to stop waiting for validation to live, to create, to rise.

"By the time they approve, the moment will have passed. Live now. Don't waste your glow waiting for permission slips from people who don't even believe in themselves."

Then she pulled me close and whispered:

"You don't need their nod. You don't need their applause. The Divine already stamped you. The ancestors already sent you. The mission is already in motion. So walk like it. Speak like it. Stand like it."

Reflection Prompt

- Where in my life have I made external validation the gatekeeper to my self-worth?
- What moments of self-trust have I ignored because someone else didn't approve or applaud?
- What would change if I accepted that I am already complete, with nothing to prove?

Write a list of every time you showed up for yourself—even when no one noticed. Let that list be your proof.

Activation Practice: Inner Completion Ceremony
Mirror Completion Mantra

Look at yourself fully in the mirror. Eyes open. Shoulders back.

Say aloud:

"I am not missing. I am not lacking. I am not waiting. I am already whole. Already divine. Already enough."

Candle + Seal Ritual

Light a candle (white or violet).

Say:

"I seal myself in truth. No opinion can undo what I am. I was sent here complete."

Completion Circle Journal

Draw a circle in your journal. Inside it, write:

"What makes me complete now?"

Then fill it in—not with achievements, but with truth. With the parts of you that always existed—courage, heart, resilience, vision, breath.

Grandma's Closing Word

"You don't need their post. Their text. Their claps. Their nod. You came here full. The world just taught you to forget. But I'm here to help you remember. You're not becoming—you're revealing. So stop searching for validation in empty hands. Everything you need? You already are."

Chapter 21: Final Words From Grandma

A Letter to Her Legacy (You)

"If you're reading this, baby…then you've made it through storms I prayed over before you were even born. And I need you to know—I'm proud of you. I've always been. I always will be."

This chapter isn't a lesson.
It's a letter.
From her heart… to yours.
From her prayers… to your path.
From her spirit… to your legacy.

My Darling, My Child, My Continuation…
You were never alone. Not even once.

Even in the silence.
Even in the confusion.
Even when the world tried to break you.
Even when you forgot who you were—I didn't.

I saw you. I prayed for you.
Every time I anointed my head,
I whispered your name into the oil.
Every time I swept the floor,
I cleared the path for your destiny.
Every time I cried, it wasn't for weakness
—it was so you would be strong.

You were chosen before you ever took your first breath.

You came here with light in your bones and fire in your feet.
And no one—not family, not friend, not fear, not foe—can undo that.

They can try. But they'll fail. Every time.
Because what's in you… was born before them.
I taught you everything I could while I had the time.
And now that I've crossed through the veil, I'm still teaching you.

In the wind.
In the warmth of your tea.
In the way your chest tightens before a bad decision.
In the peace you feel when you finally choose you.

Keep choosing you.
Keep walking like your feet are being kissed by the soil that remembers you.
Keep rising like your bloodline depends on it
—because it does.

Keep writing, even when your hands shake.
Keep praying, even when your voice cracks.
Keep shining, even when it scares the room.
Keep protecting your peace like it's breath
—because it is.

Forgive yourself faster.
Trust yourself deeper.

Rest when needed.
Laugh without asking permission.
And when they come for you, when they lie,
when they forget who you are—you remember.

Remember what I said:

You are not a rug.
You are not broken.
You are not weak.
You are not too much.
You are sacred.
You are sent.
You are complete.
You are the altar.
You are the answer.
You are mine.

I walk with you still.
When you hear the wind whisper your name
—answer back.
When you feel your heart swell for no reason
—that's me.
When you wake up and feel peace resting
on your chest—that's me again.
Not gone. Just closer than ever.
And if ever you forget...

Come back to these pages.
Read them out loud.

Let my voice wrap around you
like your favorite blanket.

Let it kiss your soul back to life.
Because you, my love, are life.
You are legacy.

You are everything
I prayed would one day bloom.
Now go on.

Live well.

Love loud.

And always—always—walk like someone
who was deeply loved by her grandmother.
Because you are.

Forever and always,
Grandma.

The Legacy Continues With You

What you've just read wasn't
just about my grandmother.
It wasn't just about me, either.
It was about you.

Your journey.
Your remembering.
Your rising.

These pages were written not
to impress—but to awaken.
Not to give you answers
—but to stir your truth.
And now that you've come this far,
I want you to pause.

Look at your life.
Look at who you've been.
Who you're becoming.
And who you're no longer willing
to abandon to make other people comfortable.
Because this is not the end.

It's the beginning of your becoming.
My grandmother didn't just raise me—
She activated a light in me that can't be put out.
She taught me how to walk tall,
even when the world wanted me crawling.

She taught me that peace is power.
That dignity is non-negotiable.
That rest is righteous.
That boundaries are holy.
That truth is enough.

And that I never needed permission to be whole.
Now, I pass that on to you.
May these pages continue to echo in your spirit every time you forget.

May her voice become your inner voice.
May your no be firm.
May your yes be sacred.
May your glow never be dimmed again—not for family, not for culture, not for fear.

This book is closed.
But the real work—the real walking
—starts now.

You've been blessed.
You've been warned.
You've been witnessed.

And now, you've been activated.
So go forward boldly,
not as a follower,
but as a firestarter,
a lineage-lifter,

a woman of her own making.

And if you ever forget again,
come back to these pages.

We'll be right here.
Waiting.

She Was the Root—I Am the Bloom

If you made it here, then you already know—
this was more than a book.
It was a reclamation.
A rising.
A ritual of remembrance.

And though every chapter carried her voice,
what I never said until now... is this:
I never met her.

Not in this world.
Not in the way most people meet
their grandmothers.

I never held her hand.
Never smelled her perfume.
Never pressed my face into
the warmth of her lap.

But I felt her—in everything.
I heard her songs before I knew her name.
I heard her prayers in my sleep.

I imagined her in the breeze, in the soil,
in the rhythm of the trees.
I pictured her in her rocking chair,
humming while I sat at her feet—

belly full from sweet mango,
sticky with coconut juice,
like my grandfather had just
come from the garden
with fruit and wisdom for me to carry.

Somewhere between breath
and memory,
between waking and dream,
she found me.

Or maybe I found her.
And if you know...
you know.

She didn't pass just to be gone.

She passed to make room for me.

She crossed over to open the road,
to leave me codes,
to whisper from beyond the veil
what the world tried to make me forget:

"You are a Gran Fanm.
A Poto Mitan.
The center pole.
The life-bringer.
The one who holds it all together."

And then she said:

"Now go and shine bright.
No one—no one—can stop you.
You are chosen.
This is not your first time.
You've saved them before.
You've healed them before.
And you're here to do it again."

So I rise.
And may you rise, too.

May the Big Spirits walk beside you.
May the Guardians protect you.

May Perfect Health and Infinite
Joy wrap around you like silk.
May all karma that is not yours stop
at your door and dissolve in the light.
May your ancestors smile every time
you speak your truth.

Whether your lineage gave you
one or eleven,
know this:
You are not alone.
You are not confused.
You are not crazy.
You are not broken.

You are the gladiator.
You are the alchemist.

You are the goddess in this realm and beyond.
You are not here to fit in.
You are here to transform.
You are a powerhouse.

A force to be reckoned with.
You come from divine lineage—
so walk like it.

And yes, much is expected of you.
Because you carry much.
You are much.

So now I leave you with this:
If only I could hug her just once…
hold her in this physical realm
and tell her thank you with
my arms instead of just my tears.

But I know this:
She lives through me.
Every step.
Every boundary.
Every time I choose myself.
So I honor her, not with grief—
but with greatness.
And I pass this blessing to you.

You were never just reading a book.
You were receiving a blessing.
Now rise.

Walk like the world is your altar.
Speak like your words are spells.

Live like you are the answer—
because you are.
And if you ever forget…

Just come back to the page.
I'll be here.
So will she.

Final Dedication

I dedicate this book to the one
who called me—
long before I even knew I was listening.

To my grandmother,
my guardian,
my whisper of warning,
my inner compass of morality,
justice, and sacred fairness.

And I dedicate this book to me—
because I could have chosen another path.
I could have ignored the nudge,
dismissed the voice,
or questioned the guidance.
But I didn't.

I listened.
I followed the divine voice.
I honored the call.
Even when no one else understood
why I was so moved…
even when I didn't fully
understand it myself—

I obeyed.
Funny, the things I know about her—
I didn't learn them from others.
I didn't need stories or records.

She told me herself.
In dreams.
In whispers.
In still moments between
thoughts and breath.
In the spaces no one could ever see.

She was always my angel,
always my truth-checker,
always my voice of reason and reassurance—
reminding me to stay pure,
to walk with empathy,
to see beyond surface and illusion.

I always seemed to know more
than I should—
knowledge that didn't belong to my age
or the experiences I had lived.

But now I understand:

She was passing it on.
From her soul to mine.
From her breath to my being.

While the world changes its mind,
its morals, and its masks,
I remain—rooted.

Because I was taught by one
who could never be swayed.

This book is for her.
This book is for me.

This book is for anyone brave enough
to listen to the voice of truth,
even when it comes from beyond the veil.

I know her name, now you write her name, and any other names that impacted your life.

_____

- -

- -

Some may have many names so here is the space to acknowledge them in this world or beyong the veil.

Aha Moment:
I Was Never Missing—Just Remembering

It didn't hit me all at once.
There wasn't a dramatic breakdown
or a bright light from the sky.
No thunder. No choir.
Just stillness.
And in that stillness, I heard her.
My grandmother.
Not with words this time—
but with presence.

She didn't say, "I told you so."

She didn't repeat the lessons.
She just was.

And in that quiet, I finally understood:
I was never broken.
I was never lost.
I wasn't "too much."

I wasn't waiting for someone to see me.
I wasn't trying to become something better.
I was returning.
To myself.
To her.
To the legacy living in my bones.

The boundary I thought was too firm?
It was freedom.

The silence I used to fear?
It was protection.
The resistance I used to fight?
It was wisdom.

Every lesson, every pain, every pushback, every pause—it was all pulling me back to this moment.
The moment where I no longer needed to search, to chase, to beg, to explain.
Because I finally saw it.

I am the altar.
I am the light.

I am the daughter and continuation of the warrior woman who never let herself be walked over, forgotten, or erased.

The power wasn't coming.
It had always been here.
It had always been me.
That's the moment everything changed.

Not because the world suddenly got softer.
But because I finally stopped asking the world for permission to be whole.

Why This Book Now, and How It Can Benefit You

This book is not a trend.
It's a timely truth.

It arrives at a moment in your life—and in the life of the world—when so many of us are tired.
Tired of the performance.
Tired of the masks.
Tired of explaining ourselves to people who don't really want to understand.
Tired of shrinking, apologizing, bending until we break.

This book was born for those moments
when you feel like your soul is whispering,
"There's more. There has to be more."
And there is.

More peace.
More self-trust.
More sacred anger that teaches you boundaries.
More softness that doesn't make you weak.
More power that doesn't ask for permission.

This book isn't here to fix you
—because you're not broken.
It's here to remind you of what's already in you.

It benefits you by handing you a mirror
that doesn't distort, manipulate, or demand.
It reflects back your sacredness.

Your worth.
Your clarity.
Your inheritance.
These aren't just Grandma's words.

They are your armor, your medicine,
your map, and your return.
Right now, the world wants
to steal your attention,
confuse your identity, and dull your light.

This book brings you home.

Back to your voice.
Back to your knowing.
Back to the rhythm of your legacy.

And once you know—really know
—you can never unknow again.

Words of Encouragement

You made it here.
That alone is proof that something
powerful is blooming within you.

So if today you feel weary, take a breath.
You are not behind.
You are not late.
You are not lacking.
You are unfolding.

And every lesson you've walked through
—every heartbreak, every silence,
every sacred no—was not in vain.

Let this book be a balm, a sword,
a warm lap to rest your head.

Let it remind you that you do not need
to be louder, smaller, sweeter, stronger,
or more "healed" to deserve peace.

You are already enough.
Even with shaky hands.
Even with a tired heart.
Even when you're still learning.

Keep rising.
Keep resting.

Keep remembering.

You don't owe this world performance.
You owe your soul presence.

And I hope you live so loudly in your truth that everything false trembles around you.

You are seen.
You are held.
You are never walking alone.

Final Declaration

*"I am not a rug.
I am not here to be walked on,
silenced, or shaped by anyone's fear.*

*I am sacred ground.
I am divine fire.
I am my grandmother's legacy.*

*I walk like a throne.
I speak like an altar.
I breathe like a prayer.*

*I am not waiting to be seen.
I see me.*

*I am not waiting to be saved.
I rise.*

*From this moment on,
I protect my peace,
my light, and my lineage.*

*I am the one.
I always have been."*

Conclusion: The Legacy Continues With You

What you've just read wasn't just about my grandmother.
It wasn't just about me, either.
It was about you.

Your journey.
Your remembering.
Your rising.

These pages were written not to impress—but to awaken.
Not to give you answers—but to stir your truth.
And now that you've come this far, I want you to pause.

Look at your life.
Look at who you've been.
Who you're becoming.
And who you're no longer willing to abandon to make other people comfortable.
Because this is not the end.

It's the beginning of your becoming.
My grandmother didn't just raise me—
She activated a light in me that can't be put out.

She taught me how to walk tall, even when the world wanted me crawling.

She taught me that peace is power.
That dignity is non-negotiable.
That rest is righteous.
That boundaries are holy.
That truth is enough.
And that I never needed permission to be whole.

Now, I pass that on to you.
May these pages continue to echo in your spirit every time you forget.
May her voice become your inner voice.
May your no be firm.
May your yes be sacred.
May your glow never be dimmed again—not for family, not for culture, not for fear.

This book is closed.
But the real work—the real walking—starts now.

You've been blessed.
You've been warned.
You've been witnessed.
And now, you've been activated.

So go forward boldly,
not as a follower,
but as a firestarter,
a lineage-lifter,
a woman of her own making.

And if you ever forget again,
come back to these pages.
We'll be right here.

Waiting.

Final Conclusion: She Was the Root—I Am the Bloom
(Repeat)
If you made it here, then you already know—
this was more than a book.
It was a reclamation.
A rising.
A ritual of remembrance.

And though every chapter carried her voice,
what I never said until now… is this:
I never met her.
Not in this world.
Not in the way most people meet their
grandmothers.

I never held her hand.
Never smelled her perfume.
Never pressed my face into the warmth of her lap.
But I felt her—in everything.

I heard her songs before I knew her name.
I heard her prayers in my sleep.

I imagined her in the breeze, in the soil,
in the rhythm of the trees.

I pictured her in her rocking chair,
humming while I sat at her feet—
belly full from sweet mango,
sticky with coconut juice,

like my grandfather had just come from the garden
with fruit and wisdom for me to carry.

Somewhere between breath and memory,
between waking and dream,
she found me.
Or maybe I found her.
And if you know… you know.

She didn't pass just to be gone.
She passed to make room for me.

She crossed over to open the road,
to leave me codes,
to whisper from beyond the veil what
the world tried to make me forget:
"You are a Gran Fanm.
A Poto Mitan. The pillars.
The center pole.
The life-bringer.
The one who holds it all together."

And then she said:
"Now go and shine bright.
No one—no one—can stop you.
You are chosen.
This is not your first time.
You've saved them before.
You've healed them before.
And you're here to do it again."

So I rise.

And may you rise, too.

May the Big Spirits walk beside you.
May the Guardians protect you.
May Perfect Health and Infinite
Joy wrap around you like silk.

May all karma that is not yours stop at
your door and dissolve in the light.
May your ancestors smile every time
you speak your truth.

Whether your lineage gave you one or eleven,

know this:

You are not alone.
You are not confused.
You are not crazy.
You are not broken.
You are the gladiator.
You are the alchemist.
You are the goddess in this realm and beyond.

You are not here to fit in.
You are here to transform.
You are a powerhouse.
A force to be reckoned with.

You come from divine lineage—
so walk like it.
And yes, much is expected of you.
Because you carry much.
You are much.

So now I leave you with this:

If only I could hug her just once...
hold her in this physical realm
and tell her thank you with my arms
instead of just my tears.

But I know this:

She lives through me.
Every step.
Every boundary.
Every time I choose myself.

So I honor her, not with grief—
but with greatness.

And I pass this blessing to you.
You were never just reading a book.
You were receiving a blessing.

Now rise.

Walk like the world is your altar.

Speak like your words are spells.
Live like you are the answer—
because you are.

And if you ever forget…
Just come back to the page.

I'll be here.
So will she.

Bonus Epilogue:
The Woman I Never Met—But Always Knew

This is the part I didn't tell you before.
The twist.
The truth.
The treasure.

You see... I never met my grandmother
in this physical world.
Not once.
Not in the ways you'd expect.

Not in photos or stories passed
through aunts and cousins.
Not in Sunday dinners or birthday phone calls.
But I know her more intimately
than I know anyone else.

She is my pulse.
She is the echo in my breath.
She is the stranger who feels like my twin.

She is the blood in my womb
and the breeze on my face.
She is the voice that told me to rise
when I had nothing left.

She is infinite wisdom—not just "good" or "bad."
She is the way.

The silence that sings.
The knowing that soothes.
The fire that heals.

She whispered into my spirit before I had a name.
She blew breath into my nostrils while I was still curled in her daughter's womb.

She knew me—before this world ever saw me.
And I know...

She didn't just leave this earth.
She laid her body down so I could rise.
She gave up space so I could have mine.

She made the path before I ever had to walk it.
I wasn't just her grandchild.
I was her continuation.
Her purpose.
Her sacred return.

She looked at me—through time, through spirit, through dimensions—and said:

"You are my daughter more than hers.
You are chosen. You are the one.
Now go and become."

To her, I could never outlive my usefulness.
I'm not a burden.

I'm her blooming.
Her prophecy fulfilled.

She told me,

"Even in the mud, you'll bloom like the lotus.
Even in the cracks, you'll be sealed with gold.
Even in heartbreak, you'll walk like royalty.
Even in abandonment, you'll remember
you are never alone."

And my God, she was right.
She covered me.
Spoke life over me.
Protected me beyond the grave.

Believed in me when I barely believed in myself.
She made me the rose from concrete,
the light from shadow,
the goddess from grief.

To the outside world, our connection
may seem mysterious.

But for those who know?
You know.
This bond isn't a fantasy.
It's not a façade.
It's the most pure, sacred,
authentic relationship

I've ever known.
She is my friend.
My shield.

My twin flame in another realm.

And today,
I realize the most divine truth of all:
I am her.
And she is me.

And if you dare come against me,
know this—
She will make you pay.
Not in vengeance, but in justice.

She is the guardian of my soul,
the melody in my silence,
the poetry of my power,
the masterpiece in my mirror.
She called me:

"Gran Fanm.
Warrior.
Poto Mitan.
Alchemist.
Gladiator.
Daughter of Light.
Healer of Timelines.
Goddess across Dimensions."

And she left me with this final command:

"Now go.
Shine brighter than they can bear.
Hold nothing back.
This world cannot contain you.
You were born for more.
You were born to be the light."

And now I know why I'm here.
To bloom.
To teach.
To live fully.

To remind others like you that
you're not alone, and you are
never too far from your power.

She taught me how to stay in the light.
And for that,
I am eternally grateful.

Final Message to the Reader:
A Love Letter to the Grandmothers

Some of you may have lost your grandmother long ago.
Some of you may have never truly known her,
or only now realize how much she was holding behind the veil.

This book...
was never just about my grandmother.
It was a mirror,
a memory,
a melody—meant to remind you
of how wonderful they are,
and how wonderful you could be.

If your relationship with your grandmother was wounded,
let this be your invitation to see her in a better light.
Not to excuse what was painful,
but to open the possibility of healing,
of understanding,
of rewriting your story with power, not pain.

And if your grandmother is still here with you in the physical?
Hug her tighter.
Hold her longer.
Listen more deeply.

Because this right here—this is a rare, living treasure.

You see…
Grandmas during the daytime are angels.
At night, they are gods.
They don't just whisper wisdom.
They reverse storms.
They lock up devils.
They shut down demons.

They know the language of prayer that no preacher can decode.

They always seem to have a solution—
a tea, a word, a stare, a silence that changes your entire perspective.

They are the breath in your body.
The steady pulse of divine rhythm.

The thread that mends the aching soul
when no one else even noticed you were unraveling.

They are the ones who
calm you after nightmares,
safeguard your spirit,
and lay hands on you when this world wants to lay harm.
And when this world tries to curse you
 with bad luck, broken homes, or heavy lineage…

It's a grandmother's prayer that cracks the curse open.
It's her love that builds a new doorway.
It's her spell that rewrites your name in light.

It's her voice that travels through time to tell the gods,
"This one is mine. This one must rise."

Even the curses that came from broken mothers—
she can break them.
Because grandmothers aren't just women.
They are frequencies.
Sacred codes in human form.

The living keys to remembering what this world tried to make you forget.

So today,
I honor not only mine…
But yours.

Whether she lives in your house, your dreams, your memory, or your bones—

Respect her.
Cherish her.
Thank her.
Call on her.
Make her proud.

She is the map to your magic.
She is the root of your healing.
She is the witness of your worth.

And if you have no one else in this world to turn to—you still have her.

Ayibobo to the grandmothers of this world.

To the warrior women who made a way.
To the ones who whispered life when no one else could.
To the ones who stayed with us—even beyond the veil.

Ayibobo to mine.

And Ayibobo to yours.

Letter to your Grandma or anyone who helped you

Letter to your Grandma or anyone who helped you

Letter to your Grandma or anyone who helped you

Notes & Aha moments.

Notes & Aha moments.

Notes & Aha moments.

Misc. Notes.

www.ingramcontent.com/pod-product-compliance
Lightning Source LLC
Chambersburg PA
CBHW070945230426
43666CB00011B/2566